A New [barcode: MW00479056]

on **EARTH**

as it is

in **HEAVEN**

Bob Lively

TREATY OAK PUBLISHERS

PUBLISHER'S NOTE

This is a work of personal memoir and inspiration. All of the characters, business establishments, and events are based on the author's personal experiences. Individuals' names may have been changed to protect their privacy.

Printed and published in the United States of America

TREATY OAK PUBLISHERS

ISBN-978-1-943658-41-1

Available in print and digital from Amazon

DEDICATION

To Mary Lynn

TABLE OF CONTENTS

PREFACE

"Mr. Lively, are you saved?"

Most every Sunday of my life from the time I was in kindergarten until I left home to attend college, I was in a Presbyterian Sunday school. Never one time do I recall any teacher talking about anyone being delivered or saved from a fiery hell. However, once I attended a backwoods brush arbor revival deep in piney woods of East Texas. A preacher armed with a microphone attached to amplifiers loud enough to be heard two counties over screamed a warning about getting right with God or else risk roasting in hellfire for all of eternity.

Distracted trying to catch June bugs, I gave her scary tirade little attention. My grandparents appeared unfazed by her fear mongering, so I decided not to listen as I crawled about in the red dirt in search of just the right bug to attach to the long piece of thread I'd lifted out of my grandmother's sewing basket. Thoughts of eternal punishment were beyond my five-year-old mind, but first capturing and then dive bombing a June bug into some farm wife's piled up hairdo definitely was not.

Consequently, as a kid growing up in a blue-collar section of Dallas, I seldom, if ever, gave the concept of Hell any real consideration. However, in high school and even in college, my friends and I would often admonish each other to venture straight to this dark netherworld either in our effort to express humor or to signal genuine anger.

To us, "Hell" was a convenient and acceptable little swear word that we used much too often to emphasize some point we thought worthy of our adolescent hyperbole. For example, we'd holler, "Let's beat the Hell out of our biggest football rivals," or we might say, "That teacher just scared the living Hell out of me."

For the most part, Hell remained an unexamined possibility that I never wanted to think about, much less believe to be a reality. And I wasn't compelled to consider it until my candidacy for the ministry required me to meet with an examination committee of the Presbyterian Church following my first year in seminary.

The kindly old pastor who chaired the committee began my examination by asking me if I believed that Jesus' death and resurrection had saved me from anything. I answered in the affirmative, stating I was convinced Christ had saved me from myself. I'm not certain what exactly I meant by this rather sophomoric response, but my answer did in the end prove satisfactory to this committee, enough that I was allowed to continue my theological education.

I'd read the New Testament in college and, of course, in seminary along with other books, such as Dante's Inferno, but still I could never quite convince myself that I believed in a literal, physical Hell. For the whole of my life I'd been taught to believe that God's very identity is love. For me, love was not something God did, but was rather who God truly is. Therefore, I could in no way understand how a God, who is absolute love, could hurl souls into the fires of Hell.

I graduated from seminary with honors, passed the ordination exams with ease, and never once gave the concept of a literal Hell much, if any, consideration. However, my careful avoidance of the topic ended one spring night during my first year of service to the church in Dallas. During the Lenten season of that year, the senior pastor sent me, along with the other associate pastors, to offer a Bible study in the homes of church members throughout the city.

I was assigned to the home of an attractive young couple I'd been warned were no nonsense, strident fundamentalists who viewed any kind of textual criticism or interpretation of Scripture as heresy. At first glance, I found it ironic to be sent to this particular home, when I had invested three years studying form criticism and, of course, biblical interpretation.

As I stepped up to the front porch with a sense of dread, I rang the doorbell with a trembling finger. The well-dressed and perfectly coifed young woman answered the door wearing an unsettling scowl. I'd been in this family's den only a few minutes before she positioned herself on a piano bench and played a series of old hymns familiar to me only by virtue of my occasional visits to a tiny fundamentalist church in the piney woods of deep East Texas.

She didn't actually play the upright piano as much as she hammered the keys, and as she sang, her shrill, slightly flat voice increased so in volume enough make my head ache. A succession of doorbell rings interrupted her pious concert, and with each ring she jumped to her feet and ran to the front door to welcome her guests with all manner of boisterous pleasantries, the kind of greeting she had denied me. Following each such reception, she would return to the piano and continue with her unrequested and unappreciated concert.

> "I suspect that is a question best left for God to answer."

The gathered guests who filled the room did what people do when they feel a little unsure in any social situation. They smiled a lot at each other and at me. Finally, she concluded her religious caterwauling with an 'amen' that could be heard a block away.

Obviously pleased with her performance, she turned to face me and smiled the kind of smile a water moccasin offers seconds before it strikes. And then she hit me with a question I suspect she'd been holding since the very first day I was introduced to the church as their new associate pastor:

"Mr. Lively, are you saved?"

Gasping at her unsolicited interrogation, I paused to consider my options. I very much wanted to treat her rudeness with a flippant response, but fortunately, I thought better of saying, "Beats the hell out of me."

Instead, I offered a more thoughtful response. "I suspect that is a question best left for God to answer."

The woman's reflexive show of anger stunned me even further. With tears welling in her eyes, she announced in an authoritative tone, "Any man who does not know he is saved is not fit to lead a Bible study in this or in any Christian home."

As her fellow church members fidgeted in their seats, she rose to her feet. "You are no longer welcome in our home. Please leave."

Of course, there was no way I could argue or protest, so I rose from my chair and made an embarrassed and silent exit from her house, no doubt leaving the small group of folks still gathered in her cozy den feeling bewildered and God only knows what else.

The next morning, feeling dejected and totally confused, I walked into my senior pastor's office and offered to resign, but this sympathetic man offered three healing words: "Consider the source."

Not only did I consider the source, but also I remained in that position for ten years, all the while wondering what I and the saints of that old church really believed regarding what it means to be saved. And since it's been more than forty years since I was unceremoniously invited to leave the home of a prominent church family, I've decided to write this book, in the cause of declaring to myself and to others what I suspect, at least, it means to be saved.

RDL

"Our vocation is not simply to be, but to work together with God in the creation of our own life, our own identity, our own destiny… to work out our identity in God."

Thomas Merton
New Seeds of Contemplation

1

THE DILEMMA OF SELF

The truth is troubling.

For the past four-and-one-half decades, I have served the church as an ordained Presbyterian minister. More specifically, I have assumed various roles within the church, including college and seminary professor, community activist, newspaper columnist, author, recovery center chaplain, teacher-in-residence at both a Baptist and an Episcopal church, a church pastor, and a professional and certified pastoral counselor.

During the course of those at-times challenging years, one constant remained: people came to me in the hope that I might be willing to hear the deepest yearnings of their oft-troubled hearts. Some arrived at my office door after giving up on psychiatry and its attendant pharmacology or on humanistic psychology and its myriad strategies for so-called self-actualization.

What these people asked me to do was to heal them in

whatever way I might accomplish such a daunting, if not altogether impossible, request. What I didn't tell them, at least not right away, is that I possess no power to heal or to change anyone from miserable to happy, and/or from addicted to clean and sober, and/or from self-loathing to self-loving. However, after some significant level of rapport and trust had been established, I did apprise them of the truth that while I could heal no one of anything, I was, in fact, well acquainted with One Who not only could, but Who was willing, and, perhaps even eager, to do just that.

Once these folks accepted the predicate of my own powerlessness, but far more importantly, of God's limitless power to heal their souls and minds, my work became relatively uncomplicated. Quite simply I approached these sessions with what a former beloved colleague was fond of calling "a listening heart."

> I possess no power to heal or to change anyone from miserable to happy…

And as I listened, I consistently affirmed their courage in the willingness they demonstrated in embracing the often-painful truths about their abusive childhoods, or about their dysfunctional families of origin, or about their troubled adult relationships. Through this process of listening and genuinely caring about them as fellow human beings, I sensed that I somehow managed, in spite of my own sinful nature and spiritual myopia, to mediate, always quite mysteriously, the Spirit's power to heal.

Once more to be clear, absolutely none of this healing came from me. It merely came through me, once I learned the art of getting out of my own way.

Soon after I became a full-time pastoral counselor, I came to realize how ill-equipped and limited my intellect was to do the work required of me. This painful awareness at times generated a very real sense of panic, making me question the lifetime of decisions that had brought me to this specialized ministry of the church. I had to admit the truth: I was a very ordinary man with nothing more than one very ordinary mind. There was nothing at all special about me, and if I possessed any real gifts, intellectual or otherwise, I was in no way aware of them.

To make matters worse, I worked with colleagues who were gifted and even brilliant. As I made the mistake of comparing myself to my colleague's obvious skills and abilities, I even viewed myself as somewhat of a fraud. And yet, people kept seeking me out in the hope I might in some substantive way help them to discover relief from whatever psychic/emotional pain plagued them at the moment.

As a consequence, it was through my own existential crisis that I discovered the truth. It is love—and love alone—that is the healing power of the human soul, as well as of the heart and of the mind. I discovered that if I loved the people who came to me seeking help, they would, in time, experience some significant measure of healing.

But along with this discovery, I further came to understand that the process of loving these people involved a paradox of sorts. The 'self' my clients presented to me to accept, if not embrace, was in reality the very source of their suffering.

In other words, the 'self' they had created in order to survive and to cope with their lives was at the same time their bulwark against this world's proverbial slings and arrows as well as their greatest problem. The 'self' they had created as a solution to this fallen world's assault upon their very being had become their problem.

It's no easy thing to convince people that they are the great stumbling block to their own happiness and or inner peace. Nevertheless, love wills us to do just that, because invariably the 'self' we create is constructed upon a foundation of existential angst.

And simply put, love's primary purpose then is to cast out fear.

As a result, it is within the process of healing that we come to discover we are required to die to the fear-based, false self we've worked a lifetime to create before we can ever hope to know any real and lasting inner-peace.

To be clear, this book is not so much about dying as it is about living. And to be more specific, it is about the amazing discovery that this life we've been given is to be lived in that glorious, realm Jesus called, "…On Earth as it is in Heaven."

Jesus gave us that oxymoron, which we now recite as part of the Lord's Prayer. Was he really raising the possibility that Earth could be like Heaven? How can we humans, flawed as we are, ever pull off something so revolutionary? We didn't learn anything about that as children in Sunday school. In fact, we likely learned the opposite.

> Love's primary purpose is to cast out fear.

The cosmic paradigm most often bequeathed to us by our elders was as simple as it was sobering. And in its simplest form, it went something like this:

1. From the very beginning God has always loved us, but unfortunately

2. We were born into a curse of sorts commonly called "original sin," which at its roots is a rather mysterious force within each one of us that compels us to do wrong, or to sin.

3. And, if we sin too much, and thereby offend God on a consistent basis, without any sincere repentance on our part, upon our death we will be cast into a fiery pit or into a lake of fire for all of eternity.

4. However, if we will only repent, meaning change our behavior, and, most importantly, accept Jesus Christ as our personal Lord and Savior, we will, upon the occasion of our death, be saved from hell and delivered by angels to some big swinging gates constructed of pearls where St. Peter himself will meet us and welcome us to a place where the streets are paved with gold. And once there, we will spend all of eternity balanced on a white fluffy cloud strumming a golden harp.

Perhaps my biggest surprise following graduation from a Presbyterian seminary concerned how many bright and highly educated adults never bothered to consider, much less question, this theological construct. No, for the most part they embraced it as unexamined truth in much the same way most of us embrace gravity as a given or the rotation of the Earth as the cause of a breath-taking sunset.

"This is what happens to little boys and girls who do wrong."

Not long after I was called to be an associate pastor on the staff of a large Presbyterian Church in Dallas, one of the church elders visited me. He shared the story of his first-grade Sunday school teacher in that very church, who more than seventy years before had instructed him and his classmates to cut out small paper figures of themselves and then print their own names upon their respective paper facsimiles.

Once they finished, she positioned a small metal sandbox in the very center of the room with the young children circled around it. She next placed a can of Sterno in the floor of the sandbox and lit it with a match. As the flame swelled and swirled before the startled children, she dangled each child's cut-out figure only inches above the flame before speaking this terrifying and unforgettable warning: "This is what happens to little boys and girls who do wrong."

I chuckled at the end of this man's horror story, but I quickly reined in my response once I realized that he didn't find his experience humorous. He then asked me what I thought of this story.

"What she did was nothing short of severe spiritual abuse," I said, "that should forever ban her from teaching in the church."

Fortunately, the man agreed after he signaled his satisfaction with a shallow sigh. He then chuckled as he shook his head. "I agree with you, son, but I sure as hell never forgot that particular lesson. In fact, it's about the only thing I remember about my earliest days in this old church's Sunday school."

Unfortunately, most pew-sitting Christians today believe that the life they've been given has far more to do with escaping God's wrath than it does with becoming new creations in Jesus Christ, as the Apostle Paul put it with such eloquence two thousand years ago.

Somehow today's preachers (especially those of the evangelical stripe) find it far easier to scare their flocks with terrifying images of fire and brimstone than they do to invite their fellow sojourners to experience what it means to live a life of radical love. To become a new creation in Christ.

During my almost half century of service, the church has not taught with any real consistency what salvation is, referring to Paul's text—"becoming a new creation"—or to Jesus' proclamation of Heaven in the here-and-now. Yet, I've come to view salvation as something wholly different from being delivered from a literal Hell..

Salvation, then, is not defined as being rescued from the fires of hell. One is saved once he or she discovers his or her true identity in God. This discovery is wholly synonymous with St. Paul's idea of becoming a "new creation in Christ."

Some would have us live on some kind of cosmic

"death row," but that's not why we were born into this world. Others try to prove their worth—either to the world or to themselves, or both—by collecting what the world envies and worships: success, influence, and fame. But if we spend our lives investing that way, we often find those cultural symbols to be profane and ultimately unholy.

"I sure as hell never forgot that lesson."

No, God gives us this life for the purpose of discovering Who God is and thereby at the same time discovering who we truly are.

Of course, this process of discovery requires the hard work of serious faith development. For without faith, we are left to fend for ourselves as we attempt to cobble together an identity capable of transporting us safely through what are, without exception, difficult lives. Those who live without faith merely exist, while those who embrace faith as God's great gift come to know first-hand the joy from experiencing genuine inner peace.

So, the question then becomes: How do we come to know God, and thereby discover who we truly are?

St. Paul answered that question for himself as well, as for the ages, by inviting us to collaborate with God in making us "new creations in Christ."

St. Paul is not inviting us to do something he was not willing to do himself. Rather he demonstrates in his very existence as a flesh and blood human being the truth proclaimed in these immortal, if at first glance, audacious words: " Be imitators of me, as I am of Christ."

I Corinthians 1: 11

Anyone who, like St. Paul, can offer such an amazing admonition has experienced salvation, and therefore, lives life one day at a time in that kingdom Jesus described as "on Earth as it is in Heaven." St. Paul then experienced his salvation following his encounter with the risen Christ on a road to the ancient city of Damascus.

> How do we come to know God, and thereby discover who we truly are?

And following that transformative experience, he devoted his life to imitating Christ and thereby, many would argue, invented a new religion we today know as Christianity. But before he could become an imitator of Christ, he had to first die to the old self, the self he had created. And like him, we, too, must die to the homemade self.

This death of the homemade self is not some easy, peaceful little demise. Rather it is an experience that leads us into the "the dark night of the soul," that terrifying region where the Divine Light finds us. Once we are found, it shepherds us into a future that resides mysteriously in the present tense.

And again, this place is what Jesus described as heaven right here and right now.

And once we begin life in this "Heaven on Earth," we discover three great truths:

1. We come to know God.

2. We come to know who we truly are.

3. We begin to realize what it means to be saved as we step for the first time into that new place Jesus called "On Earth as it is in Heaven."

This is salvation as St. Paul experienced it. He believed this salvation was intended for every human being who came to know first-hand and, always subjectively, the transformative power of the Holy Spirit. Salvation, then, is wholly synonymous with healing the soul. The word itself is derived from the same root word as salve.

Of course, there are numerous references to Hell in the Bible, but I have long regarded each such mention as either the interpolation of some ancient editor's dysphoria or of a scribe's attempt first to frighten, and then convince, early believers to endure the persecutions.

Salvation, then, is marked by the death of the false self and the birth of the new self that becomes the living, breathing expression of Christ in the world today.

That said: Hell is, indeed, very real, but it is neither some dark fiery pit, nor is it a lake on fire burning for all eternity. No, Hell is the misery we human beings either create for ourselves or have created for us, or we create to inflict on someone else.

I recall visiting inmates in the Dallas County Jail and feeling overwhelmed by the sheer number of men who were locked in small, over-crowded cages. No doubt, they languished in the excruciating anxiety from not knowing what comes next. A system over which they have absolutely no control will make decisions affecting their lives.

An old black man with a grizzled beard and snow-white hair to match summoned me to the steel bars separating us. In a tone barely audible, he whispered, "Pastor, what does the sun feel like today on a man's face? I've been in here four years now, and I cannot remember what it feels like."

Jail is Hell, and so is any kind of prison, be it constructed of steel and concrete and/or the cognitive and/or emotional disorder that is mental illness. Untreated depression is hell, as is every other untreated mood disorder. Enduring any kind of abuse is Hell, as is an addiction to alcohol or to drugs. Harboring resentments and/or rage is Hell, as is the loneliness that such demons generate.

Salvation, then, is marked by the death of the false self…

Many years ago I was invited to sit on a panel with a group of clergypersons to discuss the issue of homelessness in Dallas. A well-known downtown evangelist appeared to be set on attacking me at every juncture. Before our discussion began, he introduced himself by declaring that, "Unlike the church the Rev. Lively serves, our church in no way wishes to contribute to the problem."

His position was, of course, that feeding and providing shelter to the homeless only magnified and exacerbated the problem.

Later during the hour we shared, he once more focused on me. "The real problem here is that the Rev. Lively obviously does not have sufficient respect for the Devil. Because if he did, he'd never feed nor befriend the Devil's children."

I'd had enough of this big-haired Pharisee, so I finally rose to my feet. "Tell me, Doctor, do you believe in the

Devil?"

He jerked upright. "Well, of course I do."

Feeling somewhat emboldened, I pressed. " I do, too. In fact, I've seen him."

I glanced around at the folks seated at the conference table. "Just yesterday, I stepped out the big front door of our church on Jackson Street to discover a homeless man shooting heroin into a vein in his arm.

I once more saw the Devil.

And in that man's syringe, I saw the Devil."

One or two people nodded ever so slightly.

"And just last Sunday after worship, I found a family of three waiting for me at my office door. It didn't take long for me to learn that they were living under a bridge in a hundred dollar car. And in the desperate circumstances in which this family found themselves, I once more saw the Devil."

Before my pious adversary could attempt once more to correct my theology, I hit him with yet another question. "Sir, you say you believe in the Devil. But tell me, have you ever really seen him?"

The evangelist said in a low voice, "No, I can't say that I have."

The truth is troubling. Too often, we humans get so attached to our own subjective views and perceptual maps that we fail to discern Heaven on Earth. We don't recognize the Heaven on Earth for which Jesus prayed. We also don't identify the personal Hells we inflict on ourselves as well as on others.

2

THE WOUNDED SELF

But let's face reality.

_____

You have heard that it was said, 'An eye for an eye and a tooth for a tooth.' But I say to you. Do not resist an evildoer. But if anyone strikes you on the right cheek, turn the other also, and if anyone wants to sue you and take your cloak, give your cloak as well.

Matthew 5:38-41 a

Even the most casual reader of the above text can see that Jesus was not at all interested in retribution. In fact, it is obvious that he was wholly opposed to it.

And if the Son of God was opposed to retribution, how could there possibly be any retribution in the character of the One he called his Heavenly Father? The short and obvious answer is that there could not be.

But let's face reality. We live today in a retributive world.

From the beginning we are punished for our wrongdoing.

In my childhood, spanking was the most frequent form of punishment both at home and at school. In school, some form of shaming punished a minor infraction; however, every major infraction resulted in a trip to the principal's office where the wrongdoer would very likely be paddled.

For me, as for most children in the "boomer generation," the same was true at home. Of course, the theory behind this corporal punishment was that the ever-present threat of punishment would both civilize and socialize young children.

But what this system also accomplished was to instill in us, and in society at large, the core belief that punishment is not only good, but also of God, and at times even God's will.

Without question, the majority of us grew up believing that retribution was simply a part of what it means to be a human being. When some bully on the school playground insulted a boy's mother, that boy had to punish the offender or else risk being labeled a coward, or worse, a wimp. As a result, most of my boyhood friends thought nothing of striking a blow in the wake of defending his or his family's honor.

Today, retribution is not only a universal given; it is also big business. Currently in the United States, we have incarcerated more than 2 million souls in public prisons as well as in private for-profit ones.

Along with most Americans who were alive in 2001, I will never forget that September morning when the towers fell in New York. The megachurch I served at the time opened the doors of its chapel on that day so that any who felt compelled to do so might stop by and pray. A pastor was assigned to be present in the chapel during every hour. People did not come in droves, but the few who did trickle in expressed the sentiments of rage most all of us felt that awful day, and less than 48 hours later the President of the United States expressed the retributive thoughts of the nation.

The President stood at "Ground Zero" with his arm draped around the shoulder of a grimy, but still grinning, firefighter and spoke this threat into a bullhorn: "The people who knocked these buildings down will hear from us soon."

Of course, all America cheered. And soon enough, under his direction, we began bombing a nation that had nothing whatsoever to do with the September 11 attacks.

In retrospect, it appears obvious that our government really didn't know whom to bomb, so we launched an attached on an Arab country our leaders judged to possess the best targets. This is retribution run amok.

But let's face reality. No President who chose to follow

Jesus and turn the other cheek in such a moment could ever hope to be re-elected. And that is so because retribution, whatever form it assumes, is tightly knotted into the warp and the woof of American life. To exact retribution is to be patriotic.

I've long subscribed to the theory that our earliest caregivers form the image of God in our young, impressionable psyches. In other words, the adults who shape us as children teach us far more about God by the way they treat us than they do by the doctrine they teach us. And because most of us grew up in families who readily punished the mistakes and bad behaviors of their children, we learned to fear the retribution meted out by those in authority.

And who is more in authority than the God we are taught from the very beginning to fear?

> …retribution, whatever form it assumes, is tightly knotted into the warp and the woof of American life. To exact retribution is to be patriotic.

I was more fortunate than most because I grew up in a very loving and forgiving family. My three brothers and I were punished sparingly, and, no doubt, far less often than we deserved. But it was my maternal grandmother who was the first to teach me about what it meant to receive grace.

When I was but four years old, my parents brought me to stay for a week with her so that they, along with my older brother, could fly to Florida for a brief mid-winter vacation. Only moments before their departure, my father lifted me high to address me face-to-face.

With a no-nonsense countenance, he spoke this stern admonition. "Now Bobby, you be good. And don't you go messing with your grandmother, because she is a great lady."

With that, he lowered me to the gray slats of her wide, prairie-style front porch, turned, and descended the steps. Without hesitation, he jumped into his Frazier automobile and fired up the engine to head for the Dallas airport.

Our first day together went well enough, but by the second day I had discovered that her front doorbell sounded exactly like her telephone. Therefore, I found it great fun to ring her doorbell and then drop to my knees and peek through the front window in time to witness her answering the telephone. Three times in the same morning, I made her answer her phone only to discover a dial tone buzzing in her ear.

But in my fourth attempt to make her answer the phone, I sensed a cloud hovering above where I stood on her front porch. Busted!

Once my eyes focused through my tears, I spied my sweet grandmother, the grand matriarch of not only her family, but also of her small-town church, smiling down at me. As I awaited the sting of a fresh-cut switch, she lifted me into her arms and carried me through the front door and into her living room where she reclined into a big rocker all the while holding me close. She kissed me on my cheeks as she rocked, and then she began to hum a hymn from her small-town church.

Because I was dressed in shorts, I remained hypervigilant, all the while checking my flanks for any sign of the coming swat I knew I deserved. But no blow came. Instead she picked me up again and carried me to her kitchen where she served me a glass of cold milk and two sugar cookies.

Once I was finished with this memorable treat, she said through her smile, "Bobby, please don't ring my doorbell anymore."

That was it. That was my punishment: a glass of cold milk and two delicious sugar cookies.

I've often thought, and even on occasion claimed from a pulpit, that the moment my grandmother carried me to her kitchen was the moment I took my first communion. And I say this not because she recited anything about the snack being the blood and body of Christ.

Rather because in that unforgettable moment, I

experienced my first real taste of grace.

Of course, not every offense can be so overlooked and forgiven. We need rules and laws in the cause of preserving order in our lives and in society at large. And where laws exist, there must be some form of enforcement, and with enforcement, punishment eventually ensues.

The moment my grandmother carried me to her kitchen was the moment I took my first communion.

While writing this book, I drove through a small, lakefront resort community in the Texas Hill Country where I happened upon a billboard advertising a new church. Their sign read:

"No Rules… Just Jesus."

Smiling into the rearview mirror, I said to my wife, "It doesn't work that way."

She agreed, of course.

The core of the Old Testament is concerned with the telling of the Exodus story and its myriad implications and ramifications for ancient Israel. And it was out of the defining experience of the Exodus experience that the children of Israel received the law they would come to revere and worship for centuries to come. Of course, each law was followed by a prescribed punishment. For example, any form of adultery was to be punished by stoning.

But it was Jesus who intervened in the mob's stoning of a young woman accused of adultery. And in doing so, he did not abrogate the law, but rather, demonstrated to the cock-sure and self-righteous of every generation that grace, and not death, is God's judgment upon sin.

Perhaps grace is so difficult to accept because we human beings are so conditioned to punish others and, of course, even ourselves.

Throughout my ministry I've often wondered why we in the church are so quick in our need to punish others when it is so clear in the Gospels that punishment was not Jesus' way.

During my first year in seminary I was at first stunned, and then grieved, to listen to the horror stories of candidates for the ministry going before some church body to be examined for ordination. All too often those examinations devolved into some form of ecclesiastical hazing as opposed to any real test regarding the knowledge a candidate had acquired in seminary. Time and again, I heard of my older peers going before some church judicatory only to be humiliated and shamed for any variety of reasons.

One of my friends, a young man named Richard, who had been a strong student as well as a consistently compassionate fellow classmate, returned to the seminary following his examination before a Texas Presbytery. Several of us heard reports of the ordeal he had survived, and we sought to offer our meager support as we gathered around him at a seminary coffee table the morning following his examination.

After several hours of bombardment from all manner of questions the previous day, he had finally been asked if he believed in Hell. Upon responding that he did, he was next asked if he'd be willing to go to Hell for this Presbytery, and he wisely said, "I'd be willing for this entire Presbytery to go to Hell."

Fortunately for Richard, laughter ensued and the Presbytery finally voted to ordain him.

Following his tale of the whole ordeal, one of our friends said, "Why do they punish us? We've given three years of our lives to theological education when we could have been training for careers in other fields. And, believe me, those careers would have paid far more than this one ever will."

Another student posited the theory that those who are ordained experienced similar ordeals and therefore believe they must return the favor.

But it was Richard who offered a four-word answer

that satisfied me. He said very simply, "Only the wounded wound."

In those simple words, I discovered an insight that has remained with me for four decades. And I've seen it illustrated time and time again in the church and in the world at large. We hurt other people because we ourselves have been hurt.

Only the wounded wound.

To me, the issue is just that basic, that simple, and yet also, that profound.

And for as long as we do not allow the healing power of the Spirit's grace to make us whole, we will continue to inflict pain upon ourselves and others. Furthermore, we will not be able to view reality, and even our personal theology, except through the binary prism of reward and punishment.

But our Heavenly Father is in no way impaired and is, therefore, of course, completely whole. God, then, has absolutely no interest in punishing us, just as His Son, Jesus never punished anyone, not even the Roman soldiers who nailed him to a cross with such ceremony.

No, in fact, Jesus forgave those who killed him even while they were killing him. Luke records his dying words as, "Father, forgive them for they do not know what they are doing."

Luke 23:34

Jesus' words are his final blessing on humankind's eternal relationship with God, because if anything about us can be claimed as unassailable truth, it is this: all of us always stand in prodigious need of grace, because the painful truth is that we don't know what we are doing.

Jesus' prayer of intercession on the cross is a timeless and universal prayer which is meant to cover humanity in every age. God's grace protects us. By that same grace, we are saved from ourselves through the blood Jesus shed for each one of us while nailed to a Roman cross.

The ancient oral tradition that became Genesis is essentially etiological in that through employing myth and folk tales, it seeks to "explain" both the history and the socio/political reality in which ancient Israel found herself at the time. Its genius is that through its stories it created a theology that has endured and served humanity well for at least three thousand years.

The ancient writers who drew from the oral traditions of Israel to write the Pentateuch found themselves in exile in Babylonia, and thus naturally viewed themselves as being punished by God.

They viewed God as a punitive Deity whose wrath is

illustrated by the exile of the first humans from Eden. The destruction of Sodom and Gomorrah and "Noah's flood" offered them more proof, as well as the scattering of those who attempted to build a tower high enough to reach Heaven.

But if God is a God of wrath, how did this same God send to Earth a Son who was "the Word become flesh," among other things? Wasn't Jesus the very incarnation of mercy, the ultimate and final voice of forgiveness, and the perfect embodiment of love?

Did God's character change? Or did humanity's perception of God change?

For me, the answer is obvious, and the implications flowing from this answer are so profound as to change forever our understanding of our relationship with God. Salvation is not our deliverance from Hellfire, but is rather our experiencing the same kind of healing a Pharisee named Saul discovered on the road to Damascus.

Salvation, then, is wholly synonymous with healing.

Several years ago, I officiated the funeral for a man who was quite prominent and highly respected in Dallas. But what I, along with only a few others, knew was that this man was a recovering drug addict.

Prior to his untimely death, he had worked all 12 of the

steps of recovery with such sincerity and effectiveness that he reached the point of serving as a sponsor to a number of his fellow recovering addicts. To the few who knew him in the recovering community, he was not only the exemplar of the power of God to heal, but also a living legend. And in his church, where he was very active, he was generally regarded as a man who could be trusted, and as a faithful follower of Jesus.

To meet him was to admire him, and to know him was to love him.

Minutes after I pronounced the benediction at his funeral, a well-dressed older woman approached me and introduced herself as a friend of the family. Without hesitation she took my hand into her own and said, "Pastor, was the deceased saved?"

> Salvation, then, is wholly synonymous with healing.

Without hesitation, I said, "Absolutely."

As her eyebrows shot up, she said, "But how can you be so sure?"

"Because he had been transformed."

What she didn't realize in that moment is that she and I were speaking two different theological languages. Most likely her meaning of "being saved" involved being delivered from an eternity in a fiery Hell governed by Satan and ruled by demons.

My definition of "being saved" involved the kind of healing of the human soul that Saul experienced on a Syrian road somewhere on the way to Damascus.

Although I don't know this to be true, my hunch is that her theology was informed and shaped by the teachings of a Christian fundamentalism, which is the dominant expression of the faith in America today. This is the "God-said-it-I-believe-it-that-settles-it" view of Scripture proclaimed by televangelists every week on local and national broadcasts.

> "Don't believe everything you think."

And this, along with "the Prosperity Gospel," is the perspective of most of the fast-growing mega-churches in America today. And sadly, this is the approach that appears to attract the greatest number of people. They show up in droves.

But the problem with fundamentalism is that it eschews interpretation while it stifles curiosity. Our brains are hard-wired for interpretation, in fact, so much so that we cannot not interpret. In our waking hours, our minds are always on, interpreting in the cause of making sense of our invariably subjective perceptions.

Therefore, interpreting our view of reality is as natural to us as breathing.

When I was in seminary, I was admonished to hold a newspaper in one hand and the Bible in the other. And the reason for this is obvious. Both stand in need of daily interpretation.

Any power that seeks to squelch curiosity promotes ignorance, while it at the same time sets up its followers to be vulnerable to every charlatan who proclaims to possess God's latest message to humanity. Only in retrospect do I now see that my years of higher education were so beneficial because they not only taught me, but also encouraged me, to question everything, even the Scripture.

In short, they taught me to think critically.

And for that wonderful gift, I am forever in the debt of the many professors and teachers who gave so much of themselves so that I might feel free to follow my own curiosity wherever it leads me.

The final problem with fundamentalism is that it promotes self-righteousness and the kind of attendant arrogance that refuses love to all who are not like-minded.

Recently I happened upon a bumper sticker that struck me as beyond insightful. It read:

"Don't believe everything you think."

This wise and pithy warning instructs us to guard our minds against humanity's all-too-common sin of idolatry.

Theological idolatry works like this: we can become so attached to our belief systems and personal theologies that we quite unconsciously come to view our own unique appropriations of the mystery of God as God, Himself or Herself.

But God absolutely insists upon remaining a mystery known to us primarily by faith. And so we would be wise to keep vigilant against the strong temptation to equate our most comfortable and always-subjective impressions with holiness.

The ancient Pharisee, Saul, quite obviously worshipped his own belief system even to the point of being willing to punish, if not kill, those who happened to take another point of view. No doubt, he was so certain of his view that he was blind not only to his own insidious idolatry, but even more to his sociopathic behavior.

He knew no real compassion and he failed to practice any form of empathy whatsoever. He was so driven and so determined to force others to see God the way he did that he hurled himself into his own existential version of Hell. This man Saul must have been a terribly wounded man, because it is obvious he was so determined to wound others.

And no human being who is intent upon harming others can ever know the serenity and the joy that comes with experiencing the full fruition of Jesus' prayer: "On Earth as it is in Heaven. "

And inherent in Paul's example lies an invitation for every human being to do the same.

The fourteenth century mystic, St. Catherine of Siena, offered one of the most comforting insights I've ever happened upon: "It's Heaven all the way to Heaven, because Jesus said 'I am the way.'"

On the road to Damascus, this raging Pharisee did a one-eighty and abandoned the Hell of his own creation so that he might step into the Heaven God provided. And inherent in Paul's example lies an invitation for every human being to do the same.

But if we are to know the joy and the peace of residing in Heaven right here and right now, we must first die to the self we have invested a lifetime cobbling together, defending and always refining. And this is the most difficult and the most frightening challenge any human being can face.

So few ever risk it, while the masses seek a far easier faith where they can live out their entire lives as who they made themselves to be. Because it is far easier and safer to question nothing while they choose to believe whatever the preacher presents as truth.

No, it is far easier to view Heaven as some vague, distant reward after death than it is to take the risks required of experiencing it today, once we are delivered from the self we made up.

3

THE SELF

The short answer is that we don't.

———————————

I've yet to meet a Christian who didn't frequently pray the Lord's Prayer. Inarguably, it is the most common prayer prayed in the church, regardless of the denomination and/or theological bent.

In my youth, even high school football teams often prayed this prayer before a game. And in this particular context, I suspect we all viewed it as some kind of mystical talisman offered to invoke God to intervene in the cause of securing a victory with all its attendant glory.

In repeating this prayer, we Christians seem to have become wholly inured to its meaning. In this prayer, Jesus is teaching his disciples, as well as the rest of us, to pray for the human condition right here on Earth to become that of the holy circumstances of Heaven. This new reality he called, "the Kingdom of God," or "the Kingdom of Heaven."

In other words, Jesus is praying fervently for the future to break into our present and to transform this fallen world into a new Heaven right here on good old planet Earth.

Even while we say the words with pious hearts and heads bowed, we fail too often to discern both the daunting challenge in this seemingly impossible petition and the urgency driving this radical notion. It's far easier, not to mention safer, to recite the words and then move on with our own agendas.

Jesus Christ founded the church to be his living physical presence in this world.

The sad fact is that I have yet to meet many individual Christians who are wholly dedicated to the cause of bringing to fruition Jesus' vision of "On Earth as it is in Heaven." And the reasons for this are many, not the least being that the challenge appears far too daunting ever to be taken all that seriously. But, I believe Jesus took this prayer very much in earnest and expects his followers to do the same.

The biggest hurdle with this prayer begins with the word, "How?" How do we possibly live up to its holy expectations?

The short answer is that we don't.

And this is because the church has learned to sublimate this challenge, and thereby, remain what it's long been: a religious club. What do people find at this club that induces them to join without seeking elsewhere?

People discover the comfort that attends acceptance and a safe place where beautiful hymns are sung, where carefully crafted sermons are delivered with equal amounts skill and passion, and where prayers are spoken in unison without much real attention to what is being said. It is also a place where couples are joined in marriage, where the dead are memorialized, and where the sacraments are administered.

When I graduated from seminary, I left convinced that Jesus Christ founded the church to be his living physical presence in this world. St. Paul convinced me of this when he asked this question of the members of the church in ancient Corinth: "Do you not know that your bodies are members of Christ?"

1st Corinthians 6:15

This perspective is known as incarnational theology, and it captured my imagination when I graduated from seminary. I had served as an intern for 15 months in a church in Missouri, which for the most part strove imperfectly to be the living body of Christ in their small county seat town. This highly evolved congregation served the poor with a variety of effective ministries that liberated folks in the town's poorest neighborhoods of the hopelessness that attends poverty.

Upon graduation, I was sufficiently naïve to believe that all churches could, with the right kind of leadership, come to view themselves as St. Paul did: as the living body of Christ. Needless to say, I was a bit taken aback upon my arrival to serve a large downtown church in Dallas where I discovered these folks installing a half-million dollar organ in their beautiful sanctuary while handing out donated canned goods to the dozens of homeless people who came through their doors every day in search of their daily bread. This arrangement in no way squared with what I read in the New Testament regarding the form the church should assume.

> Was it the mission of this church to attract wealth?

When I questioned this arrangement, I was informed that this new organ would attract wealth.

Was it the mission of this historic downtown church to attract wealth? At least in the minds of those who ran this church at that time, the answer was an incontrovertible and thunderous, "Yes!"

Whatever happened to incarnational theology? "Oh,

that was merely the hyperbole of theory" and 'some pie-in-the-sky seminary drivel' that could not possibly be taken seriously in the real world," church leaders were quick to inform me.

My first assignment was to organize a young adult softball team and enter it into church-league play somewhere in Dallas. While I played on a fast-pitch church softball team throughout my youth, I could in no way motivate myself to do what I had been asked to do.

I suppose seminary "ruined" me because it taught me to take Scripture very seriously, but not literally.

I never did organize a softball team, but months later I did join with my more seasoned colleagues in founding a soup kitchen for Dallas' homeless population. Eight years later I collaborated with an Episcopal "street priest," who is a genuine saint, in founding an all-night shelter for the same population.

In addition, together we founded a battered women's shelter and a rent-free housing ministry for homeless families. And we did all of this because we were convinced that providing relief to the most vulnerable in our community was a small step toward being the body of Christ and toward bringing to fruition at least a fleeting glimpse of " On Earth as it is in Heaven."

Any church that is merely another social or service

club is not likely to inspire much, if any, real spiritual healing; nevertheless, churches which fail to take seriously Jesus' prayer, do appear to flourish simply because they are attractive places full of welcoming people who generally mean well and who are convinced that church growth is a sure sign of God's pleasure.

I've taught, preached, and served in these kinds of churches for more than four decades, and what I find these churches hold in common is a lack of clarity in their mission as well as a lack of commitment to any challenging biblical views regarding the form of the church. But with even minimum leadership, they tend to sustain their institution by thinking up clever ways to serve themselves while building new buildings and consistently congratulating themselves on being some of the nicest people anyone could ever hope to meet.

Not long ago, I stood before a large audience composed of the leaders of a particular church. They had invited me to come and spend an entire morning with them sharing my views on evangelism. I began my brief remarks with this question:

"What is your mission?"

Not one person raised a hand to answer, and following an awkward minute or two, the church's pastor attempted a vague, high-sounding, and convoluted rationale for the church's existence.

I was not at all surprised. My experience has been that most members of churches attend and support their church without really knowing what the church is about.

I began my career in a small town in Arkansas where I served as the first campus minister at one of the oldest private colleges west of the Mississippi. One beautiful Saturday afternoon, my wife sent me on a mission involving a hardware store.

While on my way down the sidewalk, I was surprised to discover a rather obese man approaching me, decked out in a red devil's costume replete with horns and a pointed tail. He balanced a hayfork on one broad shoulder, and the ridiculous grin that spread itself across his face as he got closer refused to fade even slightly.

> Seminary "ruined" me because it taught me to take Scripture very seriously, but not literally.

Every so often he would lift the fork from his shoulder and pretend to thrust it at his fellow pedestrians on the sidewalk. I recognized right away that this man was not out in public jabbing his pitchfork at his fellow townsfolk to be entertaining. No, he was out there on the sidewalk making a spectacle of himself, because he believed he was doing God's work.

With each jab he would yell, "Don't miss the revival tonight!"

He didn't choose to jab in my direction as he passed by. And I watched in fascination as he meandered on down the sidewalk, jabbing and yelling all in the cause of drumming up support for his church's latest revival.

No doubt, his efforts were sincere, but a person can be sincere and still be wrong. And any church, which attempts to reach people by scaring them with terrifying images of hell, is wholly ignoring St. Paul when he shares with an ancient congregation the truth of their identity as the living, breathing body of Christ.

And any church that views itself as the body of Christ has no real need to compose a mission statement, because their recognition of their true identity as the body of Christ defines their mission. And such a church dedicates its time, talent, and treasure to the causes Jesus thought important: healing souls while ushering into the present a future kingdom predicated upon love and God's definitions of justice.

Our English word salvation is derived from the Latin word, salus, which literally means health or healing. The original meaning of the word 'salvation' has been so misunderstood by Christians over the centuries that even today, in this the 21st Century, most Christians view it as a deliverance from Satan's fiery torment.

And this perspective conjures up a certain rigid cosmology where Heaven is somewhere up there and Hell is somewhere down there, while Earth remains squarely in the very middle. It's the place where we live and also that arena where the forces of good and the powers of evil wage a constant war over our immortal souls.

However, a far more highly evolved view is that Heaven awaits us all, because at St. John put it: "God is love…"

And no loving God would ever cast souls into a fiery pit of eternal torment, no matter what the later Gospel editors might proclaim.

But let's be clear. We do stand in need—in fact, prodigious need—of being saved. But this kind of salvation is far more faithful to the original Latin. It involves being healed, or more specifically, being delivered from the self we constructed in the cause of surviving in this world.

Curiously, this homemade self is simultaneously our most glorious achievement and our greatest problem. When I was writing a book on Psalm 23, I found myself stumped by verse 5, which reads:

"You prepare a table in the presence of my enemies."

I could in no way relate to this particular verse because I honestly could not imagine having any real enemies. I was painfully aware of people who didn't like me and of also people who, out whatever motives, did their best to injure me professionally.

You are the enemy!

But I never really viewed any of those unhappy souls as enemies. While struggling with the writing of this Psalm 23 book, I frequently enjoyed long walks down country roads in Texas Hill Country with my Labrador retriever, Margaret Ann. On one such walk, a stunning thought bubbled up out of my unconscious and stopped me in my tracks.

"You are the enemy!" The thought whispered louder than a clap of April thunder.

By the time I could return to my study, I felt close to overwhelmed by the evidence supporting this surprise insight. Whoever wrote Psalm 23 three thousand years before Freud enjoyed a rather sophisticated understanding of the unconscious mind. This is made clear in this ancient song which tells every human being that he or she must accept the Lord's invitation to sit down at God's table and face ourselves as we truly are.

This is a no-denial discipline and rigorously honest approach to healing. And the spiritual power inherent in verse five of the 23rd Psalm is replicated in the fourth Step of the twelve steps of recovery where the recovering person takes a fearless moral inventory of his or of her own life.

Simply put, we become whole only after we have dared to sit down at the Lord's Table and face all of who we are in both the conscious and the unconscious self.

And if and when we do this, we will experience the kind of spiritual healing that will make us whole.

And this healing is our true salvation, and also the first step to being faithful to Jesus' prayer of "on Earth as it is in Heaven."

4

GRACE

Only the best and the brightest.

———————————

As a young man of ancient Tarsus, Saul must have been more than a little gifted. Early in his life, he was invited to pursue a career as a Pharisee. And remarkably, he had achieved this career goal by the time he reached his mid-twenties.

The status of Pharisee in the Jewish life of his day was reserved for only the best and the brightest. To be a Pharisee was to be both highly esteemed and to be accustomed to privilege. Anyone who achieved this coveted rank had successfully committed to memory hundreds of pages of law.

And for Jews in Saul's world, the law was nothing less than God's will. Consequently, to memorize pages and pages of law was to know God's mind and God's very thoughts in every situation a human being could possibly face.

With this kind of status and the substantial cultural approbation it garnered, a young man would find it very difficult not to view himself as special, in fact, more special to an extraordinary degree than most anyone else. And to believe one knows God's will in every human situation can give rise to narcissism the way an agitated skunk can give rise to some serious stink. This perspective so contaminates a personality enough to disorder it to the point of being a monumental problem not only for the narcissist, but also for society at large.

What is genuine humility but the product of courage?

We read in his post-salvation writings of his keen awareness of his remarkable gifts and even of his once-vaulted status. But what is so astounding about this man is this: following his salvation experience, he wanted to boast only of his human frailties, or what he called his weaknesses.

Here, it is obvious that his narcissism had been healed and replaced with a genuine and appealing humility. And what is genuine humility but the product of the courageous work involved in knowing oneself as he or she truly is?

On the road to Damascus, he was anything but healed.

No, this man was a religious zealot whose extreme narcissism had devolved into full-blown sociopathy. He was quite willing, and obviously even eager, to punish, or even murder, those who happened to appropriate God in a way that was different from his own.

Saul's drive and pathological determination is illustrative of the trap many narcissists obsessed with religion fall into. And the trap is this: the overly religious unconsciously so equate their religious forms and institutions with God that they come to view these things as God.

And every time this occurs, religion gets sick, in fact, very, very sick.

And on the road to Damascus, this man, Saul, was well grounded in his religious traditions, but he was also quite sick. Wholly unbeknownst to him, his mission on that road was the very antithesis of God's will.

This man's biographer, St. Luke, tells us of what happened to Saul in these words:

> Meanwhile Saul, still breathing threats and murder against the disciples of the Lord, went to the high priest and asked him for letters to the synagogue at Damascus, so that if he found any who belonged to the Way, men or women, he might bring them bound to Jerusalem. Now he was going along and approaching Damascus,

suddenly a light from heaven flashed around him. He fell to the ground and heard a voice saying to him, 'Saul, Saul, why do you persecute me?' He asked, 'Who are you, Lord?'

The reply came, 'I am Jesus, whom you are persecuting. But get up and enter the city, and you will be told what to do.'

The Acts of the Apostles: 9.1-6,
New Revised Standard Version

This story is as instructive in what Jesus doesn't say as it is in what it tells us he did say.

Note that Jesus rejects the old ethic of an "eye for an eye" and replaces it with grace. Saul persecutes Jesus, but Jesus in no way chooses to retaliate.

No, he simply asks Saul a question and then identifies himself. And later we read that the light from heaven blinds Saul. But even here, this is grace, because following this temporary blindness Saul is able to view reality through new eyes. As a result, Saul is able to view that new reality Jesus proclaimed as "the Kingdom of God."

Jesus didn't scold or punish this man. He merely stopped him from harming others, and thereby, shined a light on a whole new way of being a radically different kind of man.

No wonder this man, Saul, was the first human being to write about grace as both a mystery and as a miracle.

While few, if any, of us are ever knocked off our feet or stopped in our tracks by grace, all of us experience grace far more frequently than we are aware. The best way, and perhaps the only real way, to view grace is to gaze into the rearview mirror of our lives.

> Even here, this is grace.

When I pause to reflect upon my life, I see grace event after grace event occurring just at the precise moment I needed it. Sufficient grace to forgive my sins and ease the attendant pain I have caused myself, and then to guide me out of the darkness.

When my younger brother Johnny was five years old, he was dedicated to attempting any feat accomplished by his two older brothers. Whenever we played tackle football with the boys in our neighborhood in an overgrown vacant lot behind our house, he would turn up, clutching a toy helmet and wearing a silent plea in his countenance.

The same was true of baseball in that same lot or in a basketball game in the driveway. He was always present on the sidelines, longing to be included. We usually invited him to join us, but there was just one problem: while Johnny was very smart, cute, and consistently kind, he was also a bit over weight and, to no one's surprise, uncoordinated.

In the summer of Johnny's fifth year, our father drove us to Colorado to experience Rocky Mountain National Park. One memorable afternoon, we rode in his big Oldsmobile just past the summit of Trail Ridge Road. Dad suddenly pulled the car to the road's shoulder and stopped to get a closer look at a herd of deer grazing on the summer tundra.

Without permission, Bill, my older brother, and I sprung open the car's back door and sprinted down the steep mountainside for an even better look. Unbeknownst to us, Johnny was right behind us doing his best to keep up.

And that's when it happened: his typical lack of agility conspired with gravity to bring him down. Sweet little Johnny fell hard, bashing his soft forehead against the sharp edge of a boulder.

Hearing his cry, I stopped my sprint in mid-stride and turned to see my precious little brother, the apple of the entire family's eye, lying on his back with blood gushing out of his forehead like a small river.

I turned once more, this time toward the highway to call to my father for help. Dad raced down the mountainside and lifted Johnny in his arms and carried him back to the Oldsmobile. My mother did her best to catch a breath as her sobs consumed her. I watched in horror as my mother carried her baby to the back seat where she cradled his wounded head in her arms.

And in that terrible moment, I was certain I was watching my sweet little brother die in my mother's arms.

But that's when grace showed up. From out of nowhere, another car rolled up behind us on the shoulder. When it stopped, a woman stepped out of the passenger side, and said, "I'm a registered nurse, and here I have sterile bandages and ammonia capsules."

From out of nowhere, grace showed up.

She handed the items to my mother with these instructions, "Take him down the mountain to Estes Park, and drive through town and past the lake, and you will see a clinic on your right. Go there immediately and ask for Dr. Mall. In the meantime, don't let him fall asleep. If he nods off, break one of these capsules open and place it directly under his nose. That will keep him awake. Now go, and go fast!"

My father not only violated the Colorado speed laws, but also quite likely the laws of physics on his way down the mountain. The physician the lady on the mountain recommended proved to be an exceptional doctor. He bandaged John's head and pronounced him well enough to return to his family and finish out our vacation.

Decades later, Johnny would become a country lawyer and a Presbyterian pastor in the smallest, still active Presbyterian church in all of Oklahoma. And for 30 plus years, he became the exemplar of the Kingdom Jesus proclaimed, in a town so small, few outside of central Oklahoma have ever even heard of it.

So who was this "miracle lady?" Was she an angel? Perhaps. I will likely never know, at least not in this life.

Grace comes to heal us.

But I can declare this with full integrity: she was an instrument of God's mysterious grace because she showed up and saved the life of a beautiful little boy who grew up to be the finest man I've ever known.

Fifty years later almost to the day, John died suddenly of a brain aneurism, and three different funerals were held because no one church in town was large enough to accommodate the crowds of mourners.

I suspect this is how grace works: As it did for Saul on the Road to Damascus, and as it did for our family on a mountainside in Colorado, it simply shows up to heal us of whatever dire condition infects our souls. Its mission is to heal us sometimes in the hidden places in our souls where we don't even realize we stand in need healing. Sometimes it shows up upon request, but in other moments it simply arrives of its own accord. It is always mysterious and invariably efficacious, and without question the most powerful force in the universe.

Jesus of Nazareth came as its very incarnation, or as St. John so eloquently put it, " the Word become flesh."

Grace comes to us as it chooses to arrive, sometimes as tender and as fulfilling as the warm embrace of forgiveness offered by someone we have injured, or it comes to us disguised as a well-supplied nurse who shows up on a mountainside to save the life of a little boy in real trouble. Other times it strikes us like lightning, or it slips silently into our souls like floodwater seeping through an earthen dam.

But always, it comes to us as an expression of the Almighty's love for us even when, and most especially when, we find it so terribly difficult to love ourselves.

Grace comes to us to heal us and, thereby, to save us from inflicting even more pain upon others or ourselves. While God is the Author of all salvation, grace is both God's instrument and Heaven's method.

All we need do is to recognize where we need it and to ask for it. But sometimes we don't even need to do that. At times, grace just shows up to blind us so that at last we can see with a new set of eyes before we take our first step into that holy new kingdom Jesus came to proclaim.

5

THE FOUR LIFE POSITIONS

The debate rages on.

_____

These three determinants shape the homemade self:

1. Genetics

2. The family of origin

3. Life experiences

When I studied psychology in college fifty years ago, I was taught that the jury was still out regarding which has the greater influence, the environment or genetics. And as far as I know, the debate rages on.

Be that as it may, we know that each factor plays a significant role in determining who we are as adults. And because we cannot change our genetic composition, we must focus our attention on the parts of us we can change. Those are determined by our environmental influences in general and our world views in particular.

> Three of the four life positions present significant problems.

Because of the powerful influences of our environment, we develop what is called a 'life position.' Essentially a life position is a pervasive perspective, which in large part determines our view of ourselves and of the world at large. As a consequence, these perspectives drive our behavior and impact our moods. While strong and entrenched, they are not intractable.

These are the four such basic life positions:

1. I love me, but I find it difficult, if not impossible, to love others.

2. I don't love me, but I will do whatever it takes to please others so they will love me.

3. I don't love me, and I have no real interest in loving anyone else. In fact, the idea of loving someone else is foreign to me.

4. I love me in many healthy ways, and I strive to love others as myself.

Even with only a cursory glance, we can see that three of the four life positions present some significant problems for the unfortunate souls who happen to hold these perspectives.

The first position listed above is the strong, yet still unconscious, predicate for narcissism. This is the life position Saul held when he was on the road to Damascus.

Unfortunately, this is also the life position many people hold today. Without question, they live with enormous, but most of the time unacknowledged, pain. They are driven to succeed out of the insatiable need for recognition and praise, and are eager to exaggerate their own accomplishments as a way of masking their loneliness and sense of isolation. They are also quick to rationalize their insensitive and even cruel behavior as the necessary toughness leadership invariably requires. And we discover them in every walk of life, even, and some might say especially, in the ministry.

A psychiatrist who taught me during my two years of training as a pastoral counselor once posited that every "tall-steeple" preacher he'd ever known was a narcissist. To be clear, he didn't say they were narcissistic disorders, but rather narcissists who had somehow managed to make it to the pinnacle of their chosen profession.

Not every accomplished person is a narcissist, but every narcissist longs to curry the praise and the general adulation that notable achievements attract. We have to look no further than our current President, Donald J. Trump, to witness a pathetic and truly dangerous demonstration of what is often termed in the media a "malignant narcissism."

I did not vote for this man, and I do not like either him or his policies. But every time he boasts of his brilliance, his enormous wealth, or his accomplishments, I find myself wondering if this man possesses even so much as a glimmer of self-awareness.

While I know many good and even enlightened people who profess to hate the man, I don't share their feelings about him. However, I very often feel some sympathy for him. I doubt any one with his extraordinary need for approval and adulation can claim any real friends. To be sure, people surround him, but they are either members of his family or sycophants. How terribly lonely he must feel.

Although I've worked in the past with two ministers who were narcissistic in the extreme, I've never known anyone who appears to be as isolated, frightened, or as wounded as our current President.

Saul of Tarsus was very likely one such man, and I say this because, unlike Trump who covered his insecurities by investing a lifetime chasing after money, Saul attempted to mask his own deep-seated insecurities by turning himself into a raging, self-righteous, religious terrorist. He would much rather murder innocent believers than admit he might be mistaken about God's movement in history.

> Not every accomplished person is a narcissist.

The second life position is the perspective involving a significant deficit in self-esteem coupled with the unhealthy emotional need to seek acceptance and approval by pleasing others. Folks in this category comprised probably 90% of the clients I saw during my twenty-five years as a pastoral counselor.

While those who came to see me were not profoundly mentally ill, in the sense of being psychotic or personality disordered, they did live and somehow cope with enough pain to motivate them to seek help. These folks were so wounded in childhood that they could not but fail to accept themselves as they are.

And because they learned early on to reject the kind of flaws innate to their very humanity, they constructed a more unconscious than conscious strategy for survival that typically consisted of two primary goals:

1. to strive for the impossible standard of perfection and

2. to invite and/or manipulate others into accepting them through such tactics as becoming an obsessive people pleaser and/or by elevating others to the status of demi-god and thereby praising them without question or discerning judgment.

The folks who compose this group are typically those whom psychology and psychiatry would term 'functional neurotics.' While they handle responsibilities and stay out of trouble, untold numbers—many more than we would probably guess—live lives of "quiet desperation," to borrow from Thoreau.

These folks are the mildly depressed, highly anxious worriers and compulsive controllers in our midst who see the glass as half empty. For them, joy is a fleeting experience, and inner-peace and genuine contentment are but a dream, while protracted periods of happiness are every bit as elusive as a monarch butterfly in autumn or a lightning bug on a hot summer night.

Often, when I speak before large audiences who only know me from my host's always kind and often exaggerated introduction, I begin by sharing some brief painful details of my own lifelong struggle with depression. Following that bit of self-revelation, I then invite members of the audience to raise their hands if they also have experienced difficulty accepting and loving themselves appropriately.

For them, joy is a fleeting experience.

Without exception, regardless of the composition of the audience, almost every hand goes up. And I've long suspected that those who don't raise their hand are merely uncomfortable with any form of self-disclosure.

Needless to say, this second life position is ubiquitous and likely universal, but for most people it is also a source of shame. In psychological terms, this unconscious life position is the seedbed for anxiety and for depression. In spiritual terms, this common error involves a very serious misunderstanding of the very nature and substance of love.

If love is "patient" and "kind," as St. Paul describes it, a severe deficit of both qualities exists in this second life position. Many people learn early in life to believe that being impatient with themselves and hard on themselves is an expression of humility.

But, in truth, this self-punishment and/or self-excoriation is not humility, but is rather a not-so-subtle form of self-abuse. We're so fearful of being perceived as arrogant and snobbish that we teach ourselves at a young age to become self-deprecating in the attempt to be viewed as genuinely humble. But again, self-deprecation is not humility, while knowing and embracing the whole truth about ourselves is.

The third life position involves a complete unwillingness to love both oneself or others. Without question, this is the most severe, and therefore dangerous, life position. Our jails and prisons are full of people who acquired this tragic life position somewhere along the way in their development

I once counseled a family whose single father was a marquee lawyer. Once the fourteen year-old son decided to act out the family's pain by "swapping" his family of origin for a gang of street kids his own age, he more or less absorbed the collective life position of his new family. As a result, he ended up addicted, homeless, and wanted by the police. By choosing the third life position, he ensured a certain destiny consisting of only two possible ends: an early death or incarceration.

> Unwilling to love is the most dangerous life position.

The third life position, then, is that of the sociopath, or what is also termed an 'anti-social personality disorder.'

Many years ago, one of our soup kitchen regulars walked through the front door toting a bright red toolbox on his shoulder. As he set the heavy box at the place where he intended to eat his lunch, I approached him and asked him where he'd gotten the box.

Chuckling, he said, "I lifted it out of the bed of a pickup parked over in the Farmer's Market."

I immediately returned to my office and called the police. Minutes later, the man was under arrest and cuffed with the stolen box confiscated. As he was pushed into the back seat of the squad car, he yelled at me, "You betrayed me!"

This is sociopathy in its most florid form.

And before I began my counseling training, I didn't really believe my fellow human beings could live life with no regard for their own wellbeing and with absolutely no real capacity for empathy regarding the feelings of others.

While this life position is not the predominant perspective, it definitely exists. Recently I received a call from a former minister in another town asking me to help him get his autobiography published. He invited me to share lunch with him in a little Hill Country BBQ joint.

I discovered he'd been out of prison for about six months following his conviction of stealing money from his church and elsewhere. Over a platter of smoked pork ribs and chicken, I offered him a few names and the phone numbers of people I thought might help him.

Days later, I received a call from a mutual friend who shared with me the tragic news that this slippery man was again conning people and stealing money at every opportunity. Once more, this is sociopathy. In our conversation, he conned me into believing that he had seen the light and was on his way to complete redemption, but, of course, his entire life was nothing more than a lie. I suspect he will either return to prison soon or I will read his name in the obituary, for such is the sad destiny of sociopaths.

His entire life was a lie.

The fourth and final life position is the perspective Jesus proclaimed, and the folks who hold this position are citizens of the kingdom of God. I've been privileged and greatly blessed to know many such people in my life.

These people are so full of genuine love that they share it freely and generously with the rest of us. They are the exemplars of St. Catherine's assertion that "It is heaven all the way to heaven…" They are heirs to Jesus' vision of "On Earth as it is in Heaven." Sometimes their expressions of love are so fervent and so radical as to plane against the very grain of our culture.

Two examples of this surprising, counter-cultural, and counter-intuitive love are:

1. The sign I once discovered on a red dirt country road on the Texas-Oklahoma border. A faded piece of cardboard stapled to a wooden staff in front of a small roadside vegetable stand read as follows:

> *The price of each item is clearly marked. And there is a money jar under the table. Take what you need, and make your own change. If you're not able to pay, take what you need and don't worry about making any payment. And to all who stop here, God bless.*

Only minutes after passing that inspiring sign, I attempted a sermon in a little Presbyterian church still clinging to life in a place long ago abandoned by just about everyone but a scattering of skinny cows. But in truth, the words I paused to read on that simple, water-stained sign were far more profound than any I proclaimed from that little church's antique pulpit.

I never met the folks who wrote that sign, and I know nothing whatsoever about them, except the following: They are saved.

And I say this not because I believe they have been delivered from the eternal torment of hellfire and brimstone, but rather because they see the world and themselves as Jesus taught all of us to perceive reality. They have experienced their salvation in this life, and surely they must be among the most blessed people on Earth because they are the happiest.

Only those who have discovered what it means to share their love with others are ever truly happy.

2. My friend, Juan was born on the border in far South Texas to a poor family more subsisting than actually living in a colonia on the outskirts of Laredo. When Juan's father could find work, he labored at the minimum wage, which in Texas at the time was no more than a couple bucks an hour.

Juan dropped out of school to apprentice in various construction trades, but like his father he worked infrequently and was paid very little when he did manage to work. When he was in his early twenties, he married a beautiful young girl from his colonia, and somehow they managed to move to Austin where the work was more plentiful and the wages better.

Very soon after his move to Austin, Juan's first daughter was born, and from that moment, she became the focus of his attention and a constant source of a joy he never imagined possible for himself. Two other daughters followed, but Juan admitted with a telling hint of embarrassment that his eldest was his favorite. She even bore his name in the feminine form: Juanita.

Somewhere along the way, Juan developed another love, this one for the bottle. In no time and with very little effort, he became a full-blown alcoholic who would spend as much time in the local bars as he did with his family. And, of course, this was the time in his life when misery replaced what had been a life marked by joy and pride.

One ordinary morning, Juan read in a Spanish language newspaper of a worship service sponsored by a local non-denominational church to be held in a tent. For reasons he professes he will never be able to explain, he decided to attend the service that very night.

I confess to feeling even a bit put off hearing about his intention to show up, because I'm far too skeptical, literate, and theologically sophisticated—not to mention much too arrogant—to be interested in any form of ecstatic Christianity. But none of these obstacles stood in Juan's way, and he entered that tent with a willing soul and an open mind.

> I know nothing about them except they are saved.

I have no idea whatsoever regarding the message he heard or what he witnessed or experienced under that big circus-like tent, but whatever it was, it forever changed him.

And to hear Juan tell it, he was saved that night in that eyesore of an evangelist's tent. He claims he answered no altar call, nor did he do anything or say anything to anyone but God. He simply walked in and sat down and opened his heart to whatever or whomever had drawn him there, and then he walked out dead certain he would never take another drink.

And I would have difficulty believing this story save for the truth that Juan has not had a drink for more than a decade. That kind of record confirms the veracity of his story. This man is not just blowing smoke, but rather is on fire with the truth that God means for us to become living and breathing expressions of divine love.

Not long after Juan's salvation experience, Juan's eldest daughter, Juanita, was visiting a friend in Waco, Texas. As his daughter and her friend were sitting in the front seat of her friend's car, a pickup truck sped by spraying bullets in every direction. Juan's daughter was struck in the head and died on the spot.

The shooter was soon apprehended and brought to trial where he was charged with murder, among other crimes. Juan and his wife attended the trial. The defendant was found guilty of murdering their beautiful daughter, who happened to be well on her way to becoming a vocational nurse.

At the sentencing phase, Juan approached the bench

with permission and pleaded with the judge to spare the man's life. "My wife and I have no interest in this man dying. There has been enough killing, so please don't give him the death penalty."

Perhaps it was Juan's pleas that persuaded the judge to spare the killer's life. Perhaps it was the mitigating circumstances of the crime that convinced him to sentence the man to life in prison, but whatever the cause, the man's life was spared.

Before departing Waco for home, Juan stopped by the McClennan County Jail to pay a visit to the man who was waiting to be transferred to the state penitentiary in Huntsville. No doubt, the convicted man was a bit taken aback to have a visit from the father of the young woman he had slain. But in this moment Juan was in no way shy. He extended his hand through the bars to shake the very hand that had pulled the trigger that killed his daughter. And in that one sacred, even holy, moment, Juan forgave the man.

Juan remained only long enough to learn that this killer had three young children of his own, and believe it or not, Juan promised to look in on his family from time to time.

Juan and his wife invited me to join them for breakfast tacos early one Christmas Eve. A colleague and I joined Juan and his family at a large round breakfast table where we shared our thoughts on the meaning of Christmas as we devoured the delicious tacos.

About two tacos into our meal, Juan excused himself before motioning for me to follow him. After donning my coat, I followed him to his pickup truck where I discovered three or four large plastic trash bags packed to capacity resting in the bed of his old truck.

"Toys." Juan offered a one-word explanation to a question I had not yet even asked.

"Toys?"

"Yes, these toy are on the way to Waco. They are Christmas gifts for the man's young children."

"What man?"

"Oh, you know, the man who killed my daughter."

All of my life, I've been to church, and I've been to seminary twice, once to earn a master's degree, and once to earn a doctorate. But on that Christmas morning in Dove Springs, a depressed blue-collar neighborhood in south Austin, Texas, I learned more theology than I ever did in church or in any classroom.

Honestly, I don't know how people like those who own

> I learned more theology from Juan than I ever did in church or in any classroom.

the vegetable stand and like Juan can love with such conviction and with such amazing freedom, but I do believe this: they must be the happiest people I've met and, then again, never met.

6

THE FIVE TOUCHSTONES OF SALVATION

Why does hitting bottom come first?

———————————

The salvation process appears to follow a pattern, which is neither rigid nor all that predictable. Even so, we can discern a distinct pattern in ancient history as well as in a roughly parallel process that takes shape in the individual lives of those who journey toward it.

Perhaps the first recorded pattern of salvation is recorded in the Book of Exodus, where we read of the travails of the children of Israel who suffered for four interminable centuries as slaves to the ancient Egyptians. These people either died young or subsisted in a dark place where hope no longer proved possible and where every thought of any kind of future brought with it an unbearable resignation. These people had little to live for except to serve their cruel masters and, perhaps, bring children into the collective misery they somehow endured.

The First Touchstone

THE BOTTOM

FOR THE CHILDREN OF ISRAEL, this was life at the very bottom, or the absolute nadir of human experience. Life could get no worse for them.

Yet bottom is where the salvation process typically begins. And this bottom experience, whatever form it happens to assume, is the first touchstone of the salvation experience.

Why does hitting bottom come first?

Because bottom is where the mind has at last been cracked open by the misery that generates pressure. It's also where the heart becomes interested, if not altogether invested, in discovering a way to escape the pain. People in recovery must hit their own kind of existential bottom before they can even begin to imagine being liberated from the soul-suffocating bondage that is addiction.

Several years ago I was invited to offer the invocation for the Texas State Convention of Alcoholics Anonymous. As I waited to ascend to the dais where the microphone was located, a man my age tapped me on the shoulder and said with a knowing grin, "Remember me?"

"I'm afraid you have me at a disadvantage," I said.

Bottom is where the salvation process begins.

He then introduced himself as a former college classmate. After shaking my hand, he delayed me a minute or two in order to share his own story of hitting bottom. His was a tale of one impressive triumph after another all the while being stalked by the ravenous, soul-devouring predator that is addiction.

The short version of his story was one of graduating from a prestigious law school with highest honors, and then making a pile of money. He was at home in his kitchen downing his final shot of bourbon for the afternoon when his exhausted and furious wife ushered their three young children out the front door of their spacious Dallas mansion with a promise of never returning. Because the shock of their long-threatened departure had now come to fruition, he felt moved to call for help. Within minutes a friend came and drove him to a meeting of A.A. that very night. And by his report, he had not tasted of spirits for more than 25 years.

If I've heard this kind of story once, I've heard it dozens of times in my years of counseling. For some, bottom is a jail cell, while for others it is divorce court, or a urine-stained mattress in a Salvation Army Detox Center. But whatever form it assumes, bottom is always a painful place to land. In fact, so excruciating as to motivate even the most recalcitrant and defensive soul to push through their fear in order to take that first crucial step toward freedom.

Scholars tell us that more than four hundred thousand Hebrew slaves may have been in Egypt at the time of the Exodus. No doubt, to a person, they were ready to be free, but the huge obstacle facing them was the daunting question: "How?"

How do we actually gain our freedom?

How do we go about pulling off this seemingly impossible revolution?

How do we raise up a leader worthy of the trust of an entire people?

These are all sound questions, which in the end, could only be answered by God. But again, these questions were not mere challenges awaiting solutions. No, they were immovable boulders blocking every possible escape route out of Egypt. These people were desperate for a solution that had long appeared impossible. Pharaoh was not about to let these people go because the system of their bondage worked well for him in keeping his own people satisfied and the economy vibrant.

The Second Touchstone

A REVOLUTIONARY IDEA

BUT THEN, A HEBREW, WHO years before as an infant had the good fortune to be raised up out of the waters of the Nile by Egyptian royalty, arrived on the scene to become a reluctant deliverer of his people. And because he chose obedience over fear, he permitted God to make him an instrument of deliverance for an entire nation.

Moses' unexpected appearance in ancient Egypt represents the second touchstone of salvation. And the real miracle in this story are not the plagues, or the Passover event, or even the parting of the Red Sea. Rather, the miracle is that an entire nation discovered sufficient faith within their own desperate hearts to follow this amazing visionary.

How do we gain our freedom?

For whenever a people find themselves hopelessly stuck, they are in desperate need of a radical new idea that brings with it not only a realistic hope, but also a visible path out of the despair. And for the children of Israel, that's exactly what Moses became to them, a new and revolutionary idea.

And the idea was the same for these ancient people as it is today for all human beings who find themselves stuck in a dark place where hope refuses to penetrate. And that radical new idea is this: there is a God who can and who will liberate a soul from

There is a God who can and who will...

whatever dark place that soul resides, if that soul will only trust and follow.

The alcoholic can be oftentimes blessed by a "moment of clarity," whereby he or she comes to see that the disease of addiction has no absolute claim upon of their soul. And with this they see that it is possible for them to achieve sobriety and, thereby, discover genuine happiness. Then they can look forward to enjoying serenity in this life for years to come.

But such awareness comes only through the power of grace. For many, grace hits them like lightning strikes a tall ponderosa pine just below the timberline. It often strikes hard, and when it does, grace changes everything as it guides them, one step at a time, or one day at a time, toward a distinct promise.

For the children of Israel, their so-called "moment of clarity" occurred when Moses appeared in their midst and reacquainted them with a promise God had made ages before with their father, Abraham. He reminded them of God's promise of progeny and also of a new land that would forever bear their name, Israel.

For the individual, this fresh idea is one of a whole new existence where love replaces a life too long driven by angst, and where inner-peace becomes the norm. And it is in this new life that one discovers the healing of his or her own soul, which means he or she is experiencing salvation in the present tense.

The Third Touchstone

CHAOS

YET, BEFORE THIS HEALING can be fully realized, one must first arrive at the third touchstone. For the Children of Israel, the best descriptor for this third touchstone is chaos. Following the parting of the Red Sea, the Children of Israel found themselves in a vast, empty wilderness where at first glance they could discover no food source and little water.

Furthermore, they entered the wilderness as a loose

confederacy of tribes with no real form of government, and no sense of shared theology to bind them. The only religion to which they had been exposed was some form of Egyptian paganism. All they possessed was a fervent hope, a passionate dream of freedom, and their trust in the leadership of a visionary holy man who claimed to speak to a God of deliverance most of them had never even heard of.

One very long time…

Even before they set off to wander about for 40 years, however, they were already lost and terrified. No wonder they fashioned a bovine god out of gold. And no wonder that from the very beginning, they carped and complained about giving up their former security for the circumstances of chaos in the wilderness.

Anxiety drove their thinking and, of course, tainted their decisions. They had no real order in their life together, no laws, no God to worship. They didn't even the have knowledge of how to worship, much less of how to go about trusting this mysterious God.

Forty years is a long time for anything, much less wandering about in an unforgiving desert. But in ancient Hebrew the words, forty years can be translated as "one very long time."

Scholars today don't really know how long they were in the wilderness, but we can rest assured that it was for one very long time. In that wilderness, God shaped them into a nation that in time would give rise to David, Solomon, Elijah, St. Paul, and even Jesus Christ himself. And in the midst of their nomadic experience, God bequeathed to them the law and then taught them to worship the God who, through them, would fulfill another promise made centuries earlier.

These were no longer the enslaved people or the lost children of Israel. Now they had become the very people whose uncommon temerity and tenacious faith eventually elevated them to the status of being a light to this world. They were the first people to embrace the hope-sustaining truth that the living God of their father Abraham is a God of deliverance.

And by pushing through their shared sense of chaos, they discovered that God means to save people. Jesus would later both amplify and individualize this truth as he reframed the world's idea of salvation as a divine gift intended for each human being's deliverance from the sin and suffering generated by the ego-driven false or homemade self.

Chaos, then, is also the third touchstone for every human being who experiences salvation. And this is so because once a person willingly dies to the former self, that person feels at first somewhat lost and ill-at-ease in the new identity of becoming a living, and yes, even sometimes vulnerable, expression of divine love. Fortunately, this discomfort is short-lived because a certain dynamic consistently rewards this new self: love begets love.

Hence, the more one expresses love in every transaction, the more one is rewarded with the receipt of love.

> Love
> begets
> love.

The Fourth Touchstone

DEATH

THE FOURTH TOUCHSTONE IS likely the most challenging of all. This one calls us to die to all that is old and binding and instead to come alive to all that is true and good about us as new creations. For the Children of Israel, this meant to forsake forever their former self-image as an oppressed and nameless people, and embrace the new realty.

They were no longer slaves, but rather the heirs to a holy covenant, and as such were destined by God to reveal to history the truth that their God was, indeed, a God of salvation. In this new identity, they would, some thirteen centuries after the exodus, become the people God would choose to give birth to the Messiah, whose very name,

Yeshua, or Jesus, in its most literal sense, means "God saves."

The Children of Israel clawed and fought their way into the land they believed promised to them, and they could not have possibly pulled this off without a strong shared sense of their identity as the children of Israel, and as heirs to a divine promise. In simple terms, they had to die to their horrendous past before they could dare hope to claim a land inhabited by other tribes. No loose confederation of former slaves could have pulled this off, but a people joined together by their belief in a divine promise certainly could and did.

But the death of their false and former self-identity was crucial to their evolution into a great nation capable of producing prophets, poets, and storytellers whose very words prepared the way for the coming of grace to every human being. For centuries, these people waxed and waned as a nation, yet somehow they kept alive both the story of their deliverance and their hope in an anointed one, or messiah, who would come to bring salvation to the world.

Even when they were carried off into exile, they clung to their identity as a delivered people. And soon after their return to their homeland, they established the synagogue movement, whereby learned rabbis were sent out throughout the entire country to teach the traditions and the law to all the people, and most especially to the young men of every village, town, and city. And it was in a local synagogue where Jesus learned his people's traditions and the law.

Each person who seeks to experience salvation must, as the Children of Israel did, also die to the former or false self. In Mark's Gospel, Jesus said: "… and those who lose their life for my sake, and for the sake of the Gospel, will save it."

Mark 8:35b

What Jesus is telling us here is that to live in Him means to die to everything we have created as our own identity, or to die to the false self. Death of the ego-driven persona we have invested a whole lifetime developing, promoting, and defending is no simple matter. St. Paul accomplished it and in doing so changed the entire course of Western civilization.

Many Christians believe Paul began his ministry immediately following his conversion experience on the road to Damascus. But this is not the case. No, after Jesus confronted him on the road to Damascus, Paul traveled to Arabia, where he remained for three years. He did not tell us exactly what he did there, but I've long suspected he embraced a discipline of unceasing prayer as a way of permitting his old self to wither away so that his new self might emerge in the very image of Christ.

When I was in seminary, I once asked a professor why seminary was a three-year program, and with a twinkle in his eye, the old gentleman said, "Because that's how long Paul remained in Arabia."

"I sure do wish he'd come home a bit sooner," I said.

The professor only chuckled. "Son, you're not alone in that sentiment."

In his letter to the Church at Corinth, St. Paul employed the helpful metaphor of human development to describe the frightening proposition of dying to the false self. He wrote:

> "When I was a child, I spoke like a child, I reasoned like a child; when I became an adult, I put an end to childish ways."
>
> *1 Corinthians: 13-11*

This metaphor is useful on several levels, because ...

1. it dramatically softens the image of dying as it presents this touchstone as a natural step in the maturation process

2. it implies a certain ubiquity in the salvation journey by framing spiritual development as something every believer in Christ must necessarily experience

3. and most importantly, it ushers the reader to the very brink of embracing the promise, which is the fifth touchstone.

St. Paul next wrote:

"For now we see in a mirror dimly, but then we will see face to face.

"Now I know only in part; then I will know fully, even as I have been fully known."

1st Corinthians 13: 12

This passage has long been interpreted, at least in my hearing, to mean that we will at last understand much, much more about the mystery of God upon our arrival in Heaven when we stand face to face with the risen Christ. Then, and only then, we will see the whole of reality clearly. In the meantime, and in this life, we are able only to see, and perhaps comprehend, the holy mystery of God's ways in a dim mirror.

"Because I feel called to serve Jesus Christ."

And I would hold fast to this interpretation, were it not for my all-too-brief encounter with a lovely young woman named Susan. Her Methodist pastor sent her to my office to discuss the idea of her attending seminary as a married mother of two young children. She arrived in my office wearing a smile that bespoke the gentility that experience has taught me is inherent in Southern women. They are accustomed to certain requisite polite amenities prefacing any substantive conversation.

However, because I was in a hurry to get on with the day's agenda silently taunting me from my desktop, I went straight to the point. "Why do you want to attend seminary?"

Her smile refused to be cowed by my abruptness, but her eyes lit up like they had been hit with a blast of neon. "Because I feel called to serve Jesus Christ," she said in a sharp, determined tone that was in no way defiant or rude. "And I need the education to do that."

As we grew more comfortable with each other, she shared with me an accomplishment about which she was most proud. She and her beloved associate pastor had collaborated in writing an adult curriculum for her church predicated upon St. Paul's image of putting away childish things. She had so enjoyed this work and had discovered such deep satisfaction in teaching this material that she decided that God was calling her to do this as a new career. And furthermore, she indicated that her husband was fully supportive of this new venture.

We never reached the point of discussing seminary during our initial meeting, but she promised to call for an appointment and to return soon so I could help her understand what was involved in a seminary education. Days later she returned, still gentle, serene, and smiling. It was then she shared that she had seen something that changed everything about her soul.

"What is it you have seen?"

"The truth," she said beaming.

I was wise enough not to probe, so we left it at that, but Susan's assertion reminded me of Pilate's revealing question to Jesus when he said, "What is truth?"

John 18:38

In that moment, I could visualize Pilate standing face to face with the ultimate truth of love made incarnate in the person of Jesus, and being totally blind to it. Like most of us, Pilate got in his own way when he said, "What is truth?" As a result, he failed to see the answer to his ridiculous question was standing before him.

But somehow my friend Susan did see it and she permitted it to change her as it shepherded her into that new place Jesus called "…on Earth as it is in Heaven."

And in that moment, I was privileged to be in the presence of a fellow ordinary human being, who, unlike most of us, had embraced the fifth touchstone of salvation, which, of course is the receiving of God's promise. Susan was peaceful, even serene, and appeared surrendered to something or Someone so high that she was content and accepting of life just as she encountered it. She made no complaints, no mention of anxiety about anything, no resentments, no thought of grudges, and certainly no blaming, nor pessimism in any of her subsequent conversations with me. Only a subtle holiness was evident in this remarkable woman.

Most of us are not good listeners.

As I shared with her the pros and cons of seminary life, she listened with consuming attention and on occasion even took notes. Very soon, I discovered I enjoyed sharing with her as honestly as I could for the simple fact that she was an conscientious listener to an extraordinary degree. I sensed from the very beginning her genuine interest in what I had to offer.

Most of us are not good listeners because we are waiting for the speaker to catch a breath so we might jump in with our own contributions. But Susan was not like that at all. She listened with what I call a "third ear." She seemed to "hear" my moods, and even the sentiments I left unsaid.

In every way a human being can be so, she was kind. Her consistent serenity made such an impact on me as that I questioned my own sense of calling, which is something I've done countless times in my career.

In one of our earliest conversations, she dropped a bomb on me by sharing that she had been battling breast cancer for more than a year. Right away, my mind kicked into a reflexive denial because, for the sake of my own selfish emotional needs, I needed her report to be untrue.

But, of course, it was true, yet she never mentioned it again, except in response to my questions regarding her wellbeing. Never once did I see her cry about being sick, nor did she appear to fear death. Throughout our shared time together, she remained peaceful, wise, and always solicitous of my health in the wake of my own diagnosis of congestive heart failure.

In all of my four plus decades as a pastor, I've yet to meet anyone who was so on fire with the truth by being to anyone's eyes not on fire at all. The two descriptors that best describe her are: "wise" and confident." She convinced me, even without trying, that she was in no way interested in being impressive or in proving anything to anyone.

I suspect such motivation in her had long ago been put away as just one of those childish things. And she was most wise in that all that seemed to interest her was expressing love. Unlike most of us, she knew how to love herself in an appropriate way without being self-absorbed at all, and often, she expressed an authentic love for her husband, and the little boy and the little girl who were their children. She professed to love most everyone she knew, and once even confessed feeling stretched a little thin because she had too many friends.

I do know this: I loved the light and the peace she brought into my office each week. And I loved the profound impact her spirit had upon my-oft turbulent soul.

Yes, this young woman had seen something that had changed not only her, but through her experience, she had also changed the world around her.

A mere month before she was to step upon the seminary campus to begin her studies, she died in a hospital in Houston, Texas. And I have no doubt—none whatsoever—that through the ordeal of chemotherapy and its attendant misery, she remained a light to all of the medical staff who treated her.

Some might posit that it was a real shame that Susan never became a minister. But those would be mistaken, because Susan was very much a minister. Through both her faith and her humility, she proclaimed the very coming to fruition of Jesus' prayer, "…on Earth as it is in Heaven."

And of course, this means Susan was in Heaven here long before she reached Heaven there.

And such is the fifth touchstone.

7

THE SIXTH AND FINAL TOUCHSTONE

We are to become heirs.

The sixth and final touchstone of our existential salvation is the miracle of the life-changing and the soul-enhancing receipt of grace. This all sounds simple enough at the first hearing, but such is not the case. This experience requires the spiritual disciplines of trust and remaining open to mystery.

The majority of us have difficulty here for two reasons:

1. We have learned that it is not always safe to trust.

2. Opening ourselves to the work of the Spirit feels somewhere between risky and, at times, even dangerous.

Nevertheless, once we have died to our former selves, St. Paul assures us that we are to become heirs to the Spirit's amazing beneficence as we receive the "fruit of the Spirit." Each fruit is a divine gift bestowed upon us, if we are open to receiving it. And again, these gifts can only come to us by first trusting God.

Of course, the first of these gifts is the great mystery that is love.

Love comes only from God because love is God's very essence. Love is not God's work so much as it is God's core identity. Love, then, is who God is and has always been and will always be. Love is God's holy essence coming both to us and then through us. To be clear, however, love does not originate in us.

We do not love because we see ourselves as good people, or even fortunate people who were fortunate enough to have been raised in functional families where love was expressed in effective, life-giving ways. No, we love because God first loved us. And we love because God bestows upon each one of us the gift of love for the expressed purpose of giving it away.

Many of the folks I've encountered both within and beyond the walls of the church are not at all convinced that God loves everyone to an identical degree. I find this disappointing. Too many people are so focused on either making it in this life—however they might define "making it"—or on making it into their own sanitized version of Heaven, that they fail to discern an important reality. God's grace is offered to each of us in equal measure, regardless of our personal circumstances.

For decades, the church I served in Dallas ignored the hunger of the homeless men and women who knocked on their door in search of their small slice of daily bread. However, all of that changed one morning in a staff meeting when a courageous associate pastor announced that he'd convinced enough elders to open a soup kitchen. Two years after it opened, this founding pastor moved on to another church. I was then assigned the duty of directing this ministry to the hungry and to the desperate of Dallas.

> Love is God's holy essence.

One morning, as I stood at the entrance to our dining room, I encountered three well-dressed professionals, two men and a woman, approaching my station at the door. It didn't take long for me to recognize their game. The men shoved the young woman into the soup kitchen's door. It was obvious, they had promised to buy her lunch, only to usher her into our dining room. As she screamed her resistance, the men howled, their laughter tinged with mockery.

Their silly prank did not so much offend me as it caused me to ponder the deeper question of humanity's all-too-frequent inability to recognize the enormous need for compassion in our world. Even more, I questioned how it is people miss seeing the pervasiveness of God's grace.

While I wondered how people could be so callous and so indifferent to their fellow human beings, I stationed myself squarely in the soup kitchen's doorway. A bit startled that I had blocked their entry, all three pranksters glared at me in indignant surprise.

"It's okay that you don't volunteer to help us with this ministry," I said, "but it's not okay that you come down here to ridicule these people or this church."

Grumbling among themselves, they strolled away.

> How do people miss the pervasiveness of God's grace?

In the more than three decades since that incident, I have often wondered how it is that people, and especially Bible-thumping people, can remain so indifferent to such obvious human suffering. Perhaps our tendency is to intellectualize the Gospel to too great an extent. In doing so, we fail to make the inextricable connection between God's love for us and a Bible filled with commandments for us to love others, and most especially, those whom Jesus once called "the least of these."

Our English word 'compassion' is derived from a Latin term, *compassio*, which literal meaning translates to "to suffer with." If I've learned anything in the past four decades of ministry, it is that most people are simply too busy, or far too self-absorbed, or far too whatever else, to make the effort or to take the risk that true compassion requires. But each time we refuse the opportunity to demonstrate genuine compassion, we miss the whole point of receiving God's love.

The experience of receiving the fruit of the Spirit appears to work like this: St. Paul's first gift of the Spirit is love, simply because love is the fount of all other gifts of the Spirit. The other gifts Paul lists in his letter to the Church at Galatia will not be received—much less claimed as our own—unless we first embrace love. But we cannot hoard love or cling to it, because love represents a paradox, of sorts. By its very nature it must be always given away. Hence, the more we give away, the more we seem to possess.

But unless we choose compassion over our strong proclivity for self-absorption, we will not be in a place to receive God's love fully. Therefore, we will fail to become the beneficiaries of the other "fruits of the Spirit" such as joy, peace, patience, kindness, and so forth.

Love, then, is the foundation of and for everything. Moreover, it is the genuine expression of the true self, and the only path either to holiness or to any real happiness in this life. The power of love was so essential to St. Paul's theology that he was inspired to write these words to the church at Corinth in his first epistle to that congregation:

> If I speak in tongues of mortals and of angels, and do not have love, I am a noisy gong or a clanging cymbal.
>
> *1st Corinthians: 13. 1*

It is not enough to receive God's love and then just say "thank you," as we move on wherever the Spirit leads us to venture. We must give away what we have received.

The implications of this are as sobering as they are searing. In a most unexpected way, compassion then becomes an issue bearing a veiled form of self-interest.

And again, this is so because for us to enjoy the full blessing that is God's grace and its attendant spiritual gifts, we must offer compassion to others. But again, precious few people understand this connection. Perhaps this explains why so many of our churches today are far more interested in church growth and its attendant increase in the size of the annual budget than they are invested in offering any kind of systematic and efficacious expression of compassion to the suffering in their local communities.

And perhaps, this is the reason why the ancient prophets demonstrate such a keen interest in justice. While serving the church in Dallas, I was assigned to preach in the early service only to discover that the lectionary directed me to the fifth chapter of the Prophet Amos, verse 24, which reads:

> *Let justice roll down like waters and righteousness like an ever-flowing stream.*

Love, by its very nature, must be given away.

Of course, I could have ignored the lectionary, but I'd been taught in seminary to remain faithful to the discipline of following this tool. So I chose to remain with this text as I pored over pages of commentaries regarding the ancient Hebraic meaning of the word 'justice.'

Nothing I read did much either to inform or to me to inspire me to preach about God's vision of justice. I had a reasonable grasp on the cultural nuances of this multi-faceted word in our world today, but nothing in my study convinced me that I knew what the likes of Amos, Hosea, and/or Isaiah were talking about when they proclaimed God's abiding commitment to justice.

Only because I knew Amos' words mentioned above

were inscribed upon the tomb of Dr. Martin Luther King, Jr., I placed a call to a fellow pastor. For more years than I'd been alive at that point, he had served as the spiritual guide to a small black congregation in one of Dallas' poorest neighborhoods, a high-crime area the police dubbed "the war zone."

I'd met this kindly older gentleman some months earlier at a community-wide gathering of area clergy and liked him right away simply because he was one of those rare people whose genuine humility served as an expression of prodigious wisdom. Such wisdom as his was so lacking in me and in other young ministers my age.

> "God's justice is love spread all around."

His name, as irony would have it, was Dr. Loud, but he was loud only in the natural quietude of his serene and humble being. Because Dr. Loud's church was much too strapped to hire any kind of receptionist, he answered my call himself. Within minutes, he invited me to join him in his study in a tiny wood-frame church more punished by a disrespectful neighborhood than by decades of weather. The little white church, an enigma in a neighborhood riddled with bars, along with all kinds of dives and joints, resembled a solitary barnacle clinging to the hull of a long-abandoned ship.

As the church's front door squeaked open when I arrived, Dr. Loud rose from his place behind an expansive desk littered with papers and stacked high with books, all of which appeared to be different versions of the Bible. Settling into an old over-stuffed chair across from his desk, I launched into the reason behind my imposition upon his morning. A broad smile spread across his face like a massive barn door was swinging open to welcome in a full day's first light. I paused long enough to give up the attempt to explain my intrusion.

Instead, I posed to him this question: "Dr. Loud, what do the prophets mean when they speak of God's vision of justice?"

In an apparent attempt to purchase himself some time to mull over my question, this wonderful old man began searching the drawers of his big desk until he located the object of his search: a tobacco pouch. After lighting his pipe, he reclined in his office chair, which appeared permanently bent backwards toward the wall and released a few puffs. "Son," he said, "God's justice is love spread all around."

Negotiating my way through the Dallas traffic all the way back to my office, I wondered how any black pastor this man's age could possibly speak of love being spread all around when I was certain he and his congregation had been subjected to countless indignities and acts of discrimination, along with myriad miscarriages of justice for the whole of their lives. How could he or any of his church members still envision a world where people were willing to follow Micah's admonition?

"… to do justice, and to love kindness, and to walk humbly with your God…"

Micah: 6.8b

Receiving love is our ultimate blessing.

While this man's vision made no real sense to me in the context of my own subjective experience in living in Dallas while working for the kingdom Jesus proclaimed, I accepted his answer. I never did discern all that much evidence of either God's or Dr. Loud's vision of justice in Dallas. But because I suspected St. Paul would have no problem with this good man's definition, I preached Dr. Loud's interpretation of justice the following Sunday, and in all of the decades that have followed, I've yet to happen upon a better interpretation of the word.

So, for the prophets, and the apostles, and, of course, for Jesus, the receipt of love is the ultimate blessing in our existence as well as our greatest hope, our most faithful guide, the source of our very origin, and ultimately, the form of our eternal future.

In short, then, love is everything, and, therefore, is all that ever really matters.

And for St. Paul it is also the first fruit of the Spirit. The other fruits of the Spirit are: joy, peace, patience, generosity, and self-control. Each one of these gifts is the product of the acceptance of God's grace, and as such, each is a distinct mark of our salvation.

What this means is nothing short of revolutionary. Those who have been delivered from the suffering of living in the false self are those among us who have been saved. And to be clear, they have been saved, not from eternal torture in some mythical lake of fire, but rather from the painful existence of a life driven by the insatiable ego.

By grace, they have discovered their own unique, true self, whose identity is a still imperfect reflection of God's perfect identity, which, of course, is love. And because of this, today and every day of their lives, these blessed people live in a place right here on Earth Jesus called "Heaven." And, consequently, for them every new day is "on Earth as it is in Heaven."

And they are the truly blessed and the happiest people on Earth.

AFTERWORD

We don't have to worry.

When Halloween descends upon Austin, Texas, each October, two very different phenomena can be counted on to occur.

The first is the wild street party on the city's Sixth Street, where most every business is a bar or some sort of live music venue. Each October 31st, as many as one hundred thousand costumed revelers descend on the few blocks that make up Sixth Street, where they consume a small ocean of alcohol before parading about on the sidewalks and in the street, showing off their latest creative costume ideas.

Each year this raucous celebration lasts until the first hours of November, at which time the city crews roll in with high pressure hoses to wash away the small mountains of debris the revelers left. No one organizes this party, and no organization sponsors it. It just bursts into being each fall, most likely because some years ago, someone thought to parade down Sixth Street wearing an outlandish costume.

The second phenomenon is the opening of what is called "Hell House." This is a Halloween "spook house" on steroids. And a large fundamentalist church sponsors this phenomenon and carefully designs it months before Halloween for the purpose of giving people brief and terrifying glimpses of Hell. The message of "Hell House" is as powerful as it is just plain wrong, and the message is this: "Get right with God, or this is to be your future."

Every year "Hell House" is featured on Austin's local news, which shows exhibit after exhibit featuring scenes of torture followed by a full chorus of miserable sinners screaming in abject agony. The purpose of "Hell House" is the worst kind of theology because it attempts to scare people into faithfulness and into holiness.

But while this is an extreme, not to mention bizarre, example of fear-based theology, the preaching of a punitive hellfire and brimstone God is alive and well in our world today. It is time for those of us who teach in today's church to give up forever the fear tactics of the past and preach a whole new view of salvation.

While writing this book, I was privileged to enjoy lunch with my oldest friend, a man who shared with me the earliest years of our childhoods. He and I were best friends as together we negotiated our way through kindergarten and first grade. Twenty or so years later, we attended the same seminary where we renewed our friendship and enjoyed together the rigors of academic life. This man went on to distinguish himself as a church pastor and then as the dean of a Presbyterian seminary.

When I mentioned to him that I was writing a book about a new way to view salvation, he said, "Our salvation is that we don't have to worry about our salvation."

I don't believe I've ever encountered a richer, yet still succinct, statement as to the power of God's grace, and I can't imagine a better way to conclude this book than by borrowing this one line from my good friend's deep reserve of wisdom.

ACKNOWLEDGEMENTS

No book can be considered helpful or even worth reading without a good editor. Fortunately, I was by God's grace able to happen upon the best in Cynthia Stone, a woman whose skills are equal to the kind of depth required for any editor to comprehend my message. I not only thank her, but I also thank God for one so brilliant, so faithful, and so generous.

After years of wrestling with publishers regarding my previous books, I decided to go with an independent publisher, Treaty Oak Publishers, right here in Austin, Texas. I cannot imagine there could be a better independent publisher anywhere. From the very beginning, these folks have handled my work with care, expertise, and, yes, even love. I'm particularly grateful to Ms. Kimberly Greyer, who designed the cover. Without question, she is the finest graphic artist I know, and her students at Austin Community College are most fortunate to study under one so gifted and so affirming.

Once more, I have imposed upon my brother, Jim Lively, to paint the cover art, and he has produced a truly magnificent cover as a gift. Moreover, I am grateful to him for a lifetime of friendship and for all the antics and adventures we shared growing up together in a happy home.

I would be remiss if I did not mention Mary Lynn, my wife of more than half a century, who on more than one occasion saved me from disaster by offering her amazing technical expertise. And this is but one small reason why this book is dedicated to her.

Finally, I thank my daughter, Sarah, for encouraging me to write again after I'd published my 11th book. And I thank my seven-year-old grandson, Henry for "interrupting" me frequently with hugs and requests to join him in some game.

ABOUT THE AUTHOR

Bob Lively is a native Texan who was born, raised, and educated in the Dallas Public schools. He is a graduate of Austin College and also of Austin Presbyterian Theological Seminary. The Presbyterian Church ordained him in 1973, and for the past four decades he has served the church as a pastor, community activist, teacher, certified pastoral counselor, campus minister, and recovery center chaplain.

He is the author of ten books of non-fiction and one novel, and is an award-winning short story writer. For 23 years he wrote a regular column in the *Austin American-Statesman*.

Today he is retired and lives with his wife, Mary Lynn, a former university associate dean, on an acre in the Hill Country west of Austin. He has been named a distinguished alumnus of both Austin College and Austin Seminary.

Made in the USA
Columbia, SC
06 December 2019

84488809R00072